THE LORD OF THE RINGS

THE FELLOWSHIP OF THE RING

Insider's Guide

BRIAN SIBLEY

An imprint of HarperCollins*Publishers*

First published in Great Britain by Collins in 2001

Collins is an imprint of HarperCollins*Publishers*
77-85 Fulham Palace Road,
Hammersmith, London W6 8JB

www.tolkien.co.uk

1 3 5 7 9 8 6 4 2

Text © Brian Sibley 2001
Photographs © 2001 New Line Productions, Inc. All Rights Reserved.
Compilation © HarperCollins*Publishers* 2001

Portions of this text have been specially adapted by Brian Sibley from his
book, 'The Lord of the Rings: The Fellowship of the Ring Official Movie Guide'.

'The Lord of the Rings', 'The Fellowship of the Ring' and the characters and the
places therein, ™ The Saul Zaentz Company d/b/a Tolkien Enterprises under license
to New Line Productions, Inc. All Rights Reserved.

'Tolkien' ™ is a trademark of The J.R.R. Tolkien Estate Limited.

The Lord of the Rings: The Fellowship of the Ring Insider's Guide is a companion to
the film *The Fellowship of the Ring* and it is not published with the approval of the
Estate of the late J.R.R. Tolkien.

The Lord of the Rings and its constituent volumes, *The Fellowship of the Ring, The
Two Towers* and *The Return of the King*, are published by HarperCollins*Publishers*
under licence from The Trustees of The J.R.R. Tolkien 1967 Settlement.

Brian Sibley asserts the moral right to be identified as the author of this work.

Photography: Pierre Vinet

The Lord of the Rings cover (page 5) by Pauline Baynes
The Hobbit cover (page 10) by J.R.R. Tolkien

A catalogue record for this book is available from the British Library

ISBN 0 00 713194 1

Printed and bound in Great Britain by
Clays Ltd, St Ives plc

CONTENTS

LIST OF COLOUR PHOTOGRAPHS

~∞ 1 ∞~

THE JOURNEY

It was going to be a long journey. The seventeen-year-old knew that he would be sitting on a train for twelve hours. He needed something to read: a book that was long enough to last the trip. He stuffed a large paperback of *The Lord of the Rings* into his bag. It was over a thousand pages long – that ought to do!

The train pulled out of the station in the New Zealand capital, Wellington, and started off on the 424 mile trip to Auckland, where the young man was going for a six-week training course. Opening his book, he began to read…

As he did so – like millions of other readers of this particular book – he was quickly caught up in the drama and excitement of the epic tale of Frodo Baggins the Hobbit, and his quest to save the world of Middle-earth from the terrible forces of the Dark Lord, Sauron.

It was a good book to read on a journey because it was itself the story of a journey – a hazardous trek which takes its central characters from home and safety into unknown lands and terrible dangers.

The train rattled on. The boy kept reading. Page after page, chapter after chapter, all filled with unforgettable adventures: thrills and terrors, heroes and monsters. Being crazy about movies and fascinated by the whole business of film-making, a thought kept going round in the boy's head: "This book would make a great movie!"

That boy was Peter Jackson, who grew up to be a successful film director. Almost twenty years had passed since he'd read that book on the train from Wellington to Auckland, but he still remembered the excitement he had felt in thinking about how the story might be turned into a film.

"As a youngster," he recalls, "I just couldn't wait

Peter Jackson: film director on location

for somebody to film *The Lord of the Rings* — because I *really* wanted to see it! But as nobody *did* I eventually decided I would have to make it myself!"

He knew it wouldn't be easy. *The Lord of the Rings* is a long book, featuring lots of extra-ordinary characters and strange creatures, set in many different places — cosy villages, mighty cities, mysterious forests and dark caves deep beneath snow-capped mountains. It also happened to be one of the most famous books of the twentieth century, which meant that millions of people had read it and would not only want to see the film but

would have very strong ideas about how it should look.

In making *The Lord of the Rings* movie trilogy, Peter Jackson began with the book and came back to it again and again. And it is with that book that our story begins...

~ 2 ~

THE BOOK

It was a really hard question: one of those impossible exam questions which schoolchildren gaze at in horror, realising that whatever the answer is *supposed* to be, they don't know it!

One young candidate simply gave up and left the page blank. Days later, an Oxford professor who was marking the exam, found that blank sheet of paper staring him in the face. At that moment, out of nowhere, a sentence popped into his head. He didn't know what it meant, but he decided to write it down. Luckily, right in front of him, was a piece of paper just waiting to have *something* written on it! "In a hole in the ground," he wrote, "there lived a hobbit..."

The professor was J. R. R. Tolkien (the initials stood for John Ronald Reuel) and the year was 1927. Some time later, Tolkien began wondering about that sentence. What *was* a hobbit? Who was *this* hobbit? And what *happened* to him?

Bit by bit, a story started to come together. The hobbit turned out to be a Mr Bilbo Baggins who lived at Bag End in the Shire, a peaceful corner of an imaginary realm called Middle-earth.

J.R.R. Tolkien in 1937

Accompanied by Gandalf the wizard and thirteen dwarves, Bilbo set off on a perilous quest in search of dragon gold. On the way, he encountered a nasty creature named Gollum and accidentally found a magic ring that could make the wearer invisible. No one, not even the storyteller, knew just how important that ring would become.

Eventually, the tale was finished and, in 1937, it was published as *The Hobbit, or There and Back Again*. So popular was the book that the publishers were soon asking the author for another. In thinking about a sequel, Tolkien began wondering about Bilbo's magic ring...

Long before the events described in *The Hobbit*, many rings of power had been forged in Middle-earth. The Dark Lord, Sauron, had made One Ring to control all the others and the people who wore them. But this One Ring had been lost – until, that is, Mr Baggins found it...

It took Tolkien another twelve years to write the story of how Bilbo's nephew, Frodo, set out into the Land of Mordor, hoping to destroy the One Ring and, with it, the power of Sauron.

The new book was called *The Lord of the Rings*. It was so long that it had to be printed in three separate volumes: *The Fellowship of the Ring*, *The Two Towers* (both published in 1954) and *The Return of the King* (published in 1955).

How *The Lord of the Rings* trilogy then became a *film* trilogy is another story altogether...

❧ 3 ❧

THE DIRECTOR

There was the spatter of machine-gun bullets and the great ape roared in pain. Perched on the top of the Empire State Building, high above New York, the angry beast lashed out at the attacking aeroplanes.

One Friday night, nine-year-old Peter Jackson was sitting in front of the television in the family home in Wellington, New Zealand, watching the film *King Kong*. As the movie ended, with the monstrous ape falling hundreds of feet to his death, Peter was filled with excitement.

"It was," he now recalls, "the first time that I felt the power of a movie, to draw you out of the real world and take you places that you would never, ever go."

Born on Halloween night, 1961, Peter Jackson was an only child with a lively imagination. He was particularly fond of fantasy comics, books, films and television shows. But nothing made a greater impact on him than *King Kong* with its story of a film-maker travelling to a remote island, capturing a huge ape and taking him back to New York: "I was totally swallowed up by the tracking of Kong and his dramatic fights with the dinosaurs! I fell in love not just with the movie, but with the way it pulled me into a fantastical world."

King Kong was an old film: it had been made in black-and-white in 1933. But, as Peter watched it, he promised himself that one day he would make his own films. "That was the night," he says, "when I realised that what I *really* wanted to do was make movies that had the same effect on other people as that film had on me."

When his parents bought a Super-8 cine-camera, Peter immediately began making little fantasy home-movies. His first ambition was to become an animator. Drawing inspiration from the creatures in *King Kong*, Peter made and animated a plasticine dinosaur for a picture about a monster that goes on a rampage and destroys a city.

By the time he was sixteen, Peter had developed a taste for shock-horror movies and decided that he wanted to make films in live action, rather than animation. Inspired by the Hammer Horror pictures made in Britain, he embarked on making a vampire movie. Several friends were talked into taking part and, as well as directing the film, Peter also starred as the vampire-slayer!

"It was based," Peter now recalls, "on the Dracula movies with Christopher Lee that I'd been watching as a teenager." Years later, Peter would cast Christopher Lee as the wizard Saruman in *The Lord of the Rings*.

When Peter left school, he went to work as an apprentice in the print industry, but he never lost his ambition to get into films. By the time he was twenty, he had saved up NZ$250 with which he bought a second-hand 16mm camera. With more help from his friends, he began making his first amateur feature-length film, called *Bad Taste*.

After four years of working every weekend, the film was finished. "It was," says Peter, "really only a home-movie, but it enabled me to quit my job and become a full-time film-maker."

Peter made several more films – *Meet the Feebles, Braindead, Heavenly Creatures* and *The Frighteners* – before starting work on a film project that he had been thinking about for almost twenty-five years: a remake of *King Kong*.

A Hollywood studio gave the go-ahead for the

Peter Jackson directing Christopher Lee as Saruman

project, scripts were written and models were made; but, before filming could begin, the studio cancelled the movie and work was abandoned. A long-held dream had died, but Peter remembered another story that had caught his imagination – that book he had read on the train all those years before, *The Lord of the Rings*.

"I still had strong memories of reading the book," says Peter, "and I still thought that it would make a great movie." But it would take a long time and involve a great many negotiations before he could even begin to think about making a film – or, as it turned out, *three* films – based on Tolkien's book.

Describing *The Lord of the Rings* project, Peter says: "Cinema-goers will find themselves in the middle of a great adventure story with a lot of action and some wonderful characters. That is what we are trying to put on screen."

And, throughout the making of *The Lord of the Rings* movie trilogy, Peter Jackson has kept in mind the feelings of excitement that he experienced as a young boy on seeing an old black-and-white movie about a giant ape. "I have tried," he says, "to capture the fascination with the

"A great adventure
story with a lot
of action..."

interweaving of fantasy and reality that began
when I was nine years old and sat, mesmerised
watching *King Kong*..."

~ 4 ~

IDEAS AND IMAGES

There are hundreds of sheets of paper, all colours of the rainbow: red, yellow, green and blue. Two purple pages are followed by one orange and six pink. The master scripts for *The Lord of the Rings*, filling three fat files of multi-coloured pages, are kept in Peter Jackson's office. Each of the different coloured pages represents a different version of that part of the script.

Peter always knew that it wasn't going to be easy. The trouble with trying to make a film of *The Lord of the Rings* is that J. R. R. Tolkien's book is known to millions of readers world-wide, all of whom have their own ideas of how the story should be told and what the characters and places should look like.

To begin with, Peter started putting together an outline of the script with his co-producer, Fran

Peter Jackson consulting 'The Book'

Walsh. They had collaborated on several of Peter's earlier films and their script for *Heavenly Creatures* had been nominated for an Oscar. But turning Tolkien's book, with all its different characters and places, into a series of three films, would take a long time to get right.

The one thing they knew, from the beginning, was that they didn't want to make what might just be thought of as 'fantasy films'. Recalling the beginnings of the project, Fran says: "The joy is that the story feels real and that was the starting place for thinking how we might adapt the book. We wanted to preserve that feeling of 'realness' and to give life and breath to Tolkien's characters."

When they had finished their outline, they were joined by Philippa Boyens, another fan of the books, who worked with Fran and Peter to produce the first of many versions of the script. Throughout the process they kept going back to Tolkien's book. "We haven't stopped reading it!" says Philippa. "There hasn't been a day when we haven't picked it up to find out how Tolkien wrote a scene or described a particular character."

Not surprisingly, Peter Jackson is anxious about how Tolkien fans will react to his films: "I have a responsibility," he says, "not to disappoint all those people who love the books. Which is why we have tried not to lose anything that we feel is key or important to the books, and why all those things that are memorable and vivid from reading the books are there in the movies."

To help create the right 'look' for the film, Peter invited two well-known artists to join the project. Alan Lee and John Howe have, between them, created hundreds of drawings and paintings based on scenes from Tolkien's writings. Their pictures have appeared as illustrations *in* books and

'Gandalf Returns to Bag End' by John Howe

on books, as well as decorating diaries, posters and calendars.

Alan lives on Dartmoor, in the West Country of Britain, and John lives in Switzerland, but both men accepted the invitation, packed their pens and pencils and set off for New Zealand. Once there, they were soon making thousands of sketches showing ideas for costumes, armour, weapons and all the buildings, from homely hobbit-holes to great cities and beautiful palaces.

"We tried to give depth to our design," says Alan, "we didn't want people to feel that it was just something that had been put together in order to make a film, but that these places really existed and had been developing over thousands of years."

Describing how they worked on the film, John Howe says: "Drawings tended to start somewhere on a big sheet of paper, and might grow in any direction that seemed right – in fact, some of our pictures ended up yards long!"

'Galadriel's Mirror' by Alan Lee

In the film's art department there are shelves stacked high with those pictures, and each and every one of them, large or small, was to have a powerful influence on how *The Lord of the Rings* now looks on our cinema screens.

～5～

CAST AND CHARACTERS

The costume wasn't quite right, the hair and make-up would have to be changed and there was the small matter of an American accent but, as Peter Jackson watched the video, he knew that he had found his Frodo.

Elijah Wood had been asked to audition for the role of Frodo Baggins in *The Lord of the Rings*, but he really wasn't too keen. Of course, the actor wanted the part, but because he lived in America, and Peter Jackson was in New Zealand, he knew he would have to audition for the director on a video tape.

Although still not twenty years old, Elijah had already appeared in lots of movies, including *Flipper* and *Deep Impact*, and he knew exactly what video auditions were like. He would be asked to

stand in front of a camera in an office and read a few lines. This was simply not good enough for Elijah; he wanted to do something more — after all, he *was* going after the part of a lifetime.

Elijah learnt some of Frodo's speeches from the book, hired the sort of costume that he thought a hobbit might wear and found a suitable country-looking setting in the Hollywood hills. Then, with the help of a friend who had a video camera, Elijah filmed a few short scenes as Frodo. "What I wanted," he says, "was something that would convey my passion for the role and for the films; something that said: 'This is me — as a hobbit!'"

Tolkien described hobbits as being about half human height with large feet that have leathery soles and are covered with curly hair. So it is not surprising that, of all the different races living in Middle-earth, hobbits are one of the most fascinating.

To begin with, they are completely original: Tolkien invented them and you won't find them in books by any other writer. But perhaps the real reason why hobbits are so intriguing is because there is much more to them than meets the eye!

Elijah Wood as Frodo   Ian Holm as Bilbo

When we first meet Bilbo, Frodo and their friends, hobbits appear to be uncomplicated, unadventurous folk who love the simple pleasures of life like food, drink, parties and fireworks. However, as the story unfolds, we discover that they are capable of having far more courage than their size would suggest. In fact, by the end of the tale, it is not wizards and warriors but hobbits who decide the fate of Middle-earth.

Frodo Baggins, in particular, is a remarkable hobbit. Small though he is, he takes on the dangerous task of carrying the One Ring into the Land of Mordor. Here, he hopes to destroy it by throwing it into the fiery heart of Mount Doom, the very volcano where, years before, it had been forged by the Dark Lord, Sauron.

Travelling with Frodo, at least for the first part of his journey, are eight companions – the Fellowship of the Ring – whose lives also become caught up with the fate of the Ring. First and foremost among them is Gandalf the wizard who, years earlier, had accompanied Bilbo Baggins on the adventure during which the One Ring had accidentally been found.

Representing the different races of Middle-earth are the Elf, Legolas; the Dwarf, Gimli; and

Orlando Bloom as Legolas

John Rhys-Davies as Gimli

two Men: Boromir, a mighty warrior from the land of Gondor, and Aragorn, the true heir to the throne of that kingdom, whom Frodo and his friends first encounter as a mysterious wandering stranger who calls himself Strider.

Completing the group of travellers are three other hobbits: Frodo's cousins Merry and Pippin, and his devoted gardener Sam, who stays loyally at his master's side to the very end of their journey.

The Lord of the Rings is full of intriguing characters who help or hinder Frodo: Lord Elrond and his daughter, Arwen; the Lady Galadriel of the elves; and the once-great wizard, Saruman.

Cate Blanchett as Galadriel

Sean Bean as Boromir

Peter Jackson knew that he needed to find just the right actors to play these parts, so that audiences would believe in them and care about their adventures.

Among the big Hollywood names in the cast are Cate Blanchett as Galadriel and Liv Tyler as Arwen. Sean Bean stars in the role of Boromir while the talented actor, poet, artist and musician, Viggo Mortensen, plays Aragorn.

Also in the cast are two British theatrical knights: Sir Ian McKellen playing Gandalf, and Sir Ian Holm as Frodo's uncle, Bilbo, the hobbit who originally found the Ring. Veteran horror movie

Christopher Lee as Saruman   Hugo Weaving as Elrond

star, Christopher Lee CBE, is Saruman; British character actor, John Rhys-Davies (well known as Harrison Ford's side-kick in the Indiana Jones movies), is Gimli the dwarf, and Australian actor Hugo Weaving (from *The Matrix*) plays the wise Elrond Half-elven.

Alongside Elijah Wood as Frodo Baggins, Peter Jackson cast another young American leading man, Sean Astin, as Frodo's faithful companion, Sam Gamgee.

Sean, who began making movies with the teen adventure film *The Goonies*, is fascinated by the characters of Sam and Frodo: "Here are these innocent, little, big-footed people who are facing larger than life obstacles. Except that I don't think the hobbits see themselves as being 'little' until they are standing next to something that's daunting and intimidating. So we've tried to approach them as real and human as possible."

Describing the special relationship between Frodo and Sam, Sean adds: "Sam loves Frodo and wants to protect him, and Frodo is extremely protective of Sam. They find themselves locked into this journey together and they really don't

Viggo Mortensen as Strider   Liv Tyler as Arwen

need to talk about what they are to each other – they just *are*!"

The other central characters are played by comparative newcomers to the film business, like Orlando Bloom who was cast as the elf-prince, Legolas. "Tolkien's elves," says Orlando, "are nothing like the traditional image of pixies and fairies: they have great physical and mental strength, and are powerful, full-blooded people."

Orlando was still at drama school when he auditioned for the part of Boromir's brother, Faramir, who is introduced in the second film, *The*

Two Towers. Six months later, he was invited to audition again – this time for the part of Legolas. Shortly afterwards, he got a phone call offering him the role. "It was amazing!" he says. "It was like having all your dreams fulfilled!"

Interestingly, Orlando was not the only actor to be offered a completely different role from the one for which he originally auditioned. Dominic Monaghan, who was already well-known to British television viewers from the series *Hetty Wainthropp Investigates*, originally read for the part of Frodo.

Dominic had been a fan of Tolkien's books ever since his father introduced him first to *The Hobbit* and then its sequel. "Dad described *The Lord of the Rings* as a challenge," he recalls, "but said that it was well worth reading and he was right!"

Shortly after the audition (he was, he says, "really excited and really nervous!") Dominic was offered the role of Merry (full name, Meriadoc Brandybuck), Frodo's second cousin and childhood companion who becomes a member of the Fellowship of the Ring.

"Merry," says Dominic (who at 5' 7" is

Billy Boyd as Pippin, Dominic Monaghan as Merry and Sean Astin as Sam

"officially the tallest hobbit"), "is really just one of the lads! He's charming and cheeky!" With his best friend, Peregrin Took – known as Pippin – Merry has many exciting and frightening adventures. "As the journey unfolds," says Dominic, "Merry finds himself in situations where he has to look after people or make decisions that a hobbit would never normally have to make."

Describing the characters of Merry and Pippin, Dominic adds: "They are really the wild cards in the pack and the spice in the Fellowship!" It is a view shared by Scottish actor, Billy Boyd, who plays Pippin: "It's not possible to speak about Pippin without mentioning Merry. They are just the closest of friends, closer than family, so that you really can't imagine either of them doing anything without the other!"

There were many different routes by which actors came to play their roles in *The Lord of the Rings*: Ian McKellen was offered the role of Gandalf after Peter Jackson and co-producer Fran Walsh met the actor in London; Christopher Lee, who – after a lifetime in movies – never normally auditions for a part, agreed to read one of Saruman's scenes for Peter and Fran; and one reason why Ian Holm was invited to play Bilbo was because, some years before, he had played Frodo in a major BBC Radio dramatisation of *The Lord of the Rings*.

For Viggo Mortensen, the deciding factor was his son, Henry. Viggo was offered the important role of Aragorn after filming had already begun in New Zealand with another actor in the part.

"Basically," says Viggo, "I got a call asking if I wanted to go to New Zealand for fourteen months to film *The Lord of the Rings*. And my first reaction was: 'No!'"

Viggo had heard of Tolkien's *The Lord of the*

Ian McKellen as Gandalf

Rings and knew just how famous it was, but he hadn't read the book or seen the film scripts. Since there wasn't much time to prepare for what was obviously a major role, and he didn't like the thought of being away from his family for over a year, he decided to turn down the offer.

But his son had other ideas: "Henry said I was crazy," recalls Viggo. "He said that I'd *got* to do it, even if I was going to be gone a long time. So the next thing I knew I was on the plane for New Zealand reading that enormous book and, a couple of days later, I was filming!"

For the later films, *The Two Towers* and *The Return of the King*, several other major characters would have to be cast, among them Gollum. This pathetic but dangerous creature whom Bilbo met in *The Hobbit*, reappears in *The Lord of the Rings* and has a vital role to play in the final chapters of the story.

With the cast complete for *The Fellowship of the Ring*, the next task was to create the world in which their adventures would take place...

❧ 6 ❧

LOCATIONS AND SETS

To begin with, it was only a light rain. The film crew for *The Lord of the Rings* was on location, filming a scene in which the Fellowship are travelling through Middle-earth. The rain kept falling, but director Peter Jackson kept the cameras rolling. The actors trudged along getting wetter and wetter. Then the wind got colder and, suddenly, it wasn't raining any more – it was *snowing*!

Peter decided to continue filming in the hope that he might get some shots for a sequence in the first film where the Fellowship struggle through a driving snow-storm. However, real weather is impossible to control and, before long, everyone was soaking wet and freezing cold, and filming was finally abandoned for the day.

Unpredictable weather was just one of the hazards of location-filming in New Zealand. But everyone involved with the film would say that they were worth it in order to have captured the wild and beautiful landscapes which provide the amazing settings for the film.

Heavy weather on location

"New Zealand is gorgeous!" says Elijah Wood, playing Frodo. "I don't think there's anywhere else we could have filmed this movie unless we had travelled to lots of locations around the world. There are so many different landscapes: mountains, woods, marshes, desert areas, rolling hills – and the sea. Everything, in fact, described in *The Lord of the Rings*."

Orlando Bloom, who plays Legolas, remarks: "New Zealand really and truly *is* Tolkien country!"

A whole year before filming began, Peter Jackson travelled across both the North and South Islands of New Zealand, choosing the seventy locations – from dense forests of lush vegetation to towering volcanic mountains – that would be used during the filming of the trilogy.

Occasionally, the director found what he was looking for right on his doorstep: the sequence in which the hobbits hide from the sinister Black Rider was shot in the woods on the steep sides of Mount Victoria in Peter's birthplace, Wellington.

Many different locations proved to be within reasonable travelling distance from the studios in Wellington. However, a lot of the chosen sites were in conservation areas and the film-makers had to get special permission before they could move in with their truckloads of people and equipment.

Several important locations, such as the icy mountain slopes where Frodo almost loses the ring in the snow, were impossible to reach by road, and helicopters were used to fly in the actors and camera crews.

One of New Zealand's spectacular mountain landscapes

The Lord of the Rings is the story of a journey on which the characters travel through many lands, visiting towns and cities inhabited by men, the ancient kingdoms of elves and dwarves and, at last, the terrible land of Mordor itself, the stronghold of Sauron. Each of these places has an importance in the telling of the tale. As supervising art director, Dan Hennah, notes: "The settings in Tolkien's books are not backgrounds, they are very much a part of the story."

Bree

Rivendell

Those settings include the town of Bree, where the hobbits first encounter men and where they are pursued and attacked by Sauron's Black Riders; the safe haven of Elrond's house in Rivendell; the dark and dangerous Mines of Moria, deep beneath the Misty Mountains, and the Golden Wood of Lothlórien, home of the elven-queen, Galadriel.

Each place has its own distinctive look, from the narrow, muddy streets and tall, dark buildings of Bree, which loom over the little hobbits, to the light and airy rooms at Rivendell, where trees grow up through the rooms and open walls look out on to mossy rocks and waterfalls.

These mysterious and magical places were created using sets built in real locations, matched with shots of incredibly detailed miniature models and sequences filmed in studios.

The journey that leads the characters to all these places begins at Hobbiton in the Shire, where Bilbo and Frodo Baggins have their home, Bag End. It is one of the earliest locations to be seen in *The Fellowship of the Ring,* and one which every reader of *The Hobbit* or *The Lord of the Rings* will already have strong impressions as to how it should look.

The ideal setting was found, by chance, on a piece of farmland near the city of Hamilton. It took imagination to see it as the Shire, because it was a rather swampy area with nothing on it but a few trees and one or two sheep. Peter Jackson walked around the farm with artists Alan Lee and

Hobbiton

John Howe, who then sat down, got out their sketch-pads and started drawing.

"They began," remembers Peter, "by drawing the landscape we were looking at; then they added little hobbit-holes and cabbage-patches, washing-lines and hedges. I literally watched them bringing Hobbiton to life on paper. At that point I knew we had found the ideal location."

Much had to be done, however, to transform the ten-acre site into the Shire. The first essential was a proper road so that vehicles carrying costumes, equipment, catering and up to 400 people could travel in and out of the area each day.

When the road was completed, with help from the New Zealand Army, diggers and excavators began shifting 5000 kilolitres of earth to create the hills into the sides of which the hobbit-holes of Hobbiton, with their round doors and windows, would eventually be built.

Flowers and vegetables were planted in the Hobbiton gardens, fields were ploughed, hedges were created, the swamp was drained and a stone bridge was built across a small lake so that Gandalf could drive his horse and cart through the village on his way to visit the Bagginses of Bag End.

An enormous oak tree – covered with 250,000 hand-painted leaves and artificial acorns – was moved into place above Bag End. Around another *real* tree, they created the Party Field, the site of Bilbo's great birthday party, at which he would literally 'disappear' from the Shire for ever.

Bilbo's birthday party

Hobbit-holes

All this work was done a year before filming began so that the trees and plants had time to look as if they had always grown there. The buildings also began to take on the 'weathered' look of a village that has existed for hundreds of years.

"We wanted to leave enough time," remembers Peter Jackson, "for Hobbiton to become a *real place*." So it did; as did all the strange and wonderful places that are described in Tolkien's book and which were recreated on film.

~ 7 ~

PROPS AND WEAPONS

It is only a ring: a plain, gold ring. But it is the most powerful ring in Middle-earth: the One Ring belonging to the Dark Lord, Sauron – the Lord of the Rings.

The Fellowship of the Ring, like any film, required a great many 'things'. There were all the characters' personal belongings, whether swords or magic-staffs, and all the objects seen on the different sets, such as books on shelves and cups and plates on tables. Film-makers call these 'props' (short for 'properties') and they all have to be bought, borrowed or made.

"The Ring," says Richard Taylor of the New Zealand special effects company Weta Workshop, "is a very interesting prop, because it is so powerful, so fundamental to the story, but such a simple ring." Director Peter Jackson agrees; in fact, he calls the ring "the real villain of Tolkien's story".

Specially made by a New Zealand jeweller, the Ring is one of several thousand props exclusively crafted for *The Lord of the Rings* movie trilogy.

Big tankards for little people

There were three-legged stools, woven rugs and pottery mugs for Bag End, pewter tankards for The Prancing Pony Inn at Bree, glass goblets for the elves at Rivendell and hand-made leather saddles for the great heroes who ride into battle.

Quite a number of props had to be made to two scales: at the inn at Bree, tables, chairs, bottles, jugs and plates all had to look normal when used by the men of the village but look over-large when used by hobbits. Even the fish, fruit and vegetables seen on the stalls in Hobbiton had to be big enough to be in scale with the size of the actors playing the hobbit villagers.

There was also a huge armoury of swords and shields, knives and daggers, as well as pikes, axes, bows and arrows. Tolkien artist John Howe designed swords that would look quite different from the type of weapons usually seen in movies. "Film swords," says John, "are nearly all big, ugly, blunt things that you would never be able to lift if they were actually made of metal. We wanted to design and make swords that were graceful and beautiful, and that could be handled in the way *real* swords are handled."

The swords used by Aragorn and the other warriors in the film are very elaborate, with exquisitely decorated hilts and mystical elven inscriptions on their blades. These weapons were made by sword-smith Peter Lyons, employing identical techniques to those used hundreds of years ago.

Gimli wields one of his axes

There were also 'stunt swords' with aluminium blades. Every day, five copies of each actor's sword would be standing by in case a weapon got bent or broken in a fight sequence.

The armies of extras, who are seen fighting in the huge battle scenes in the later films, had swords made out of semi-rigid rubber, painted the colour of steel so that they looked completely realistic. Two thousand of these rubber swords were produced and used by actors in the background, who were then able to bash away at one another without causing damage to actors or swords!

Some particularly unpleasant weapons were designed for the vicious orcs serving in the armies of Sauron and Saruman. (Continued on page 65)

Some carry heavy cross-bows and pouches of bolts; others have stubby, oblong swords ending in a cruel upturned hook, while those referred to in Weta Workshop as 'Berzerkers' have a 'balled fist mace' that fits over the hand and is covered with lethal spikes.

A great many people were involved in designing, finding and making the hundreds of thousands of props in *The Lord of the Rings*, personally supervised by Peter Jackson. "Peter looked at each and every prop before it was seen by the camera," remembers supervising art director, Dan Hennah. "There wasn't a sword, a saddle, a flag or a spear that he didn't see and approve."

He also gave a lot of thought to the Ring. "Every time we showed it," says Peter, "I would film it in a close-up, so that it seemed much bigger. It's just a regular-sized ring and yet I wanted to make people feel the power that makes it more than just a piece of metal on somebody's hand."

～ 8 ～

COSTUMES AND ARMOUR

Sometimes it was a hat. Sometimes it was more of a nightmare! Everyone knows what a wizard's hat looks like and it is exactly like the one that Gandalf wears! A tall, pointed cone with a big, wide brim.

Some years ago, Tolkien artist John Howe made a painting of Gandalf wearing just such a hat and as soon as Peter Jackson saw that picture, he knew that was precisely the kind of hat he wanted to see Gandalf wearing in his films of *The Lord of the Rings*.

However, for costume designer Ngila Dickson, and actor Ian McKellen (who had to *wear* it), Gandalf's hat really was a nightmare!

Ngila remembers how every time she looked at John Howe's painting, she thought what a very silly idea it would be to try and make a hat like that! However, eventually it *was* made and the actor got to try it on. "I know Tolkien described Gandalf as

wearing a tall, pointed hat," says Ian, "but how tall is *tall*?"

Ngila knew that the hat was going to be a challenge: "When we first presented Sir Ian with the hat," recalls Ngila, "I really don't think he knew how to make it work, because it is really asking an awful lot of an actor to have to act from under the brim of an enormous, pointy hat!"

Not only that, but it was constantly knocking against something inside the set for Bilbo's hobbit-hole at Bag End and, on windy locations, it was always threatening to blow away!

Gandalf's hat was just one of many challenges facing the costume designer. There would be no less than twenty main characters in the three films, dozens of minor characters and thousands of extras. Also, because *The Lord of the Rings* is the story of a group of people making a long journey which takes them through woods, over mountains and across rivers, the characters needed several changes of costume in order to show the wear and tear that clothes would go through on such a journey.

The director and designer were in complete agreement that they *didn't* want fantasy costumes. They wanted clothes that looked *real* and 'lived-in', as if the characters had owned them – and worn them – for several years.

Elven costumes

Ngila began by designing the costumes for the hobbits which were knitted and woven in 'country' colours, such as green, brown and yellow. "How do you make a costume work," Ngila found herself asking, "when the characters have got big ears and big feet?" The answer, as she puts it, was to "mess with what was normal": jacket-sleeves and trouser-

Hobbit clothes

bottoms were made just a bit too short, waist-lines and pockets just a little too high. And the result was a decidedly 'hobbity' look!

In fact, each group of characters in the story had their own very individual look: for the dwarves it was a "solid, chunky, leathery" look in dark, earthy colours, while for the elves it was more "shimmery, light and airy" using materials that were pale green, grey and silver.

While Ngila and her team created the costumes, Weta Workshop was producing over 1000 suits of authentic-looking armour for the films' battle sequences. The designs were inspired by John Howe, an expert on medieval armour and weapons. John thinks that most of the armour seen on the cinema screen is completely unrealistic.

"Watch old historical movies," he says, "and you will see people dressed up in outfits that look like

Orcs dressed for battle

the one worn by the Tin Man in *The Wizard of Oz!*
As for the armour in fantasy films, that's usually bad
enough to make you ask for your money back!"

An amazing collection of armour has been
designed for the three films. Particularly impressive

Dwarf armour: solid and chunky

is the leaf-shaped leather
armour worn by the high
elves in the historical 'flash-
back' scenes where they are
seen fighting the armies of
Sauron. In contrast, Sauron's
orcs wear jagged, spikey
armour and helmets that,
around the studio, were
given names describing

their grotesque appearance, such as "crowfaced",
"squinter" and "trapjaw".

Once the armour had been designed, it had to
be *made* and Richard Taylor, the director of Weta
Workshop, decided that this would be done using
medieval skills and techniques.

"We set up a foundry with a furnace," says
Richard. "We employed two armour-smiths and
they created the armour by hand-beating it out of

plate-steel in exactly the same way as it would have been created in times past."

When all the suits of armour had been built, silicon moulds were made of the various parts. Using a polyurethane spraying machine, 48,000 separate pieces of armour were mass-produced in a plastic material that was light enough for the actors to wear for the long hours involved in filming.

Some people worked with hammers and anvils, others with needles and thread, but together they produced an amazing collection of costumes from dwarf armour to elvish dresses, to that troublesome wizard's hat!

From the moment Peter Jackson saw the finished version of Gandalf's hat, he thought it was perfect. In fact, he liked it *so* much, he decided that Gandalf should wear it in several more scenes than had originally been planned!

As for Ian McKellen, he knew that, despite the problems, Gandalf's hat was an important part of his character. "He lived with it and worked with it," recalls Ngila Dickson, "and *somehow* he managed to beat it into shape!"

❧ 9 ❧

MAKE-UP AND BODY PARTS

There is a large box filled with pairs of feet! Hobbit feet: battered and grubby, rather like old, shabby trainers! They are just a few of the 2200 feet that were made for the actors playing the

hobbit characters in *The Lord of the Rings*.

The art of making artificial body parts to change an actor's appearance is called 'prosthetics'. In addition to hobbit feet, you will see characters in *The Lord of the Rings* with prosthetic ears, noses, hands and – in the case of the fearful orcs who serve Sauron – *entire heads and bodies*!

The box of feet is in a corner of Weta Workshop,

Tania Rodger and Richard Taylor with orc heads

the company run by Richard Taylor and Tania Rodger which also created special effects for many of Peter Jackson's earlier movies.

Weta Workshop is named after a large New Zealand insect (like an overgrown cricket) that has been around for one hundred million years and is virtually indestructible! Richard Taylor is passionate about Weta's contribution to *The Lord of the Rings*. "We have not been making a movie," he says, "we have been creating a legacy!"

Visiting the workshop, which is filled to overflowing with everything from entire forests of scaled-down trees to rooms stacked with swords and shields, it is easy to understand what Richard means. Tania Rodger recalls: "It was a different world: creatures, weapons and suits of armour everywhere! There were days when the moment you came through the workshop door, you thought: 'I'm here! I've arrived in Middle-earth!'"

Weta Workshop was responsible for adding much of the magic to *The Lord of the Rings* movie trilogy: they made all the miniature scale models used to create breathtaking views of Elrond's house in Rivendell, Saruman's tower at Isengard and the elves' tree kingdom in Lothlórien. Weta was also responsible for all the armour and weapons used in the dramatic battle sequences, as well as all those pointy elf-ears, hairy hobbit-feet, rotten orc-teeth – and *Gandalf's nose!*

Quite a few noses were tried on Ian McKellen before they arrived at the 'right' one! It took some time for the actor to get used to looking in the mirror and seeing someone with a different nose looking back at him – not to mention the long hair, bushy eyebrows and beard he was given, to fit Tolkien's description of the wizard! "Eventually," says Ian, "I got used to seeing Gandalf and not myself. It's rather like changing your voice, or your walk, or the way you think!"

For Ian McKellen, the process of being

Ian McKellen being made-up as Gandalf

transformed into Gandalf would begin at around seven o'clock in the morning and last between two and three hours. For some of the other actors, it was much worse! Make-up sessions for John Rhys-Davies, playing Gimli the dwarf, began at *four* o'clock in the morning and lasted six hours! The reason it took so long was because John's whole face (except for his eyes and mouth) had to be covered in prosthetic make-up! "Fantastic part!" he says. "Wonderful character. But, in terms of make-up, a real killer!"

It was also hard for the make-up artists on the days when they had to get the orc armies ready for battle scenes. "Some days," says Richard Taylor, "we were dressing as many as 200 people in full head-to-toe body prosthetics!"

Turning the hundreds of extras on the film into rampaging armies of orcs was no easy task. Their arms and legs had to be covered with latex limbs with bulging muscles and knobbly, warty skin.

These suits were hot and uncomfortable and, after several wearings, were so sweaty and smelly that the only thing they were fit for was being fed into a shredder! Orc faces

John Rhys-Davies after 6 hours in make-up

varied depending on their race: greeny-grey skins with reptile nostrils and large, pale eyes for the goblin-orcs living in the dark of the Mines of Moria, and darker-skinned creatures with yellow cat's-eyes and sharp, jagged fangs for the soldiers of Sauron.

Fierce orc make-up including false fangs

One of the most elaborate make-ups was that created to show the birth of an Uruk-hai, a special breed of orc. This particular make-up marathon took *ten hours*! Beginning at midnight, the actor was encased in an entire body-suit (unable to see, hear or speak) and then smothered with goo and ooze! The make-up was finished just in time for filming to begin at ten o'clock the following morning.

In contrast, it only took the hobbits two-and-a-half hours to get into their wigs, ears and feet. "The first day," recalls Elijah Wood, playing Frodo, "I thought: 'This is so cool! I've got prosthetic feet!' But after a week it was: 'OK, I'm tired of this now!'"

Once they had their feet on, the hobbit actors couldn't move until the make-up artist had finished disguising the line where rubber foot met human leg. "It was strange," says Billy Boyd, playing Pippin, "having to stand still with your own feet inside *another* pair of feet! Still, I did manage to read quite a few books!"

Frodo: fully made-up

Dominic Monaghan, playing Merry, describes his hobbit feet: "They were just slightly bigger than our normal feet – and hairy! Even though they had a thick layer of latex underneath to protect the feet and keep the wet out, they were still pliable enough to walk in – or even *run* in!"

Sean Astin (Sam), remarks: "Wearing hobbit feet really *does* make you walk differently." And this is something Ian Holm discovered to his cost: "I think Bilbo Baggins' feet must have been bigger than

anybody else's!" he recalls. "I was forever tripping over them and nearly falling flat on my face!"

Dangers and difficulties aside, by the time they finally walked on set, all of the hobbit-actors felt as if they really *were* the characters. "Once we were in our gear," says Sean, "and our ears were bigger and our feet were bigger, it was quite easy to stop thinking of yourself as a human and start thinking of yourself as a hobbit."

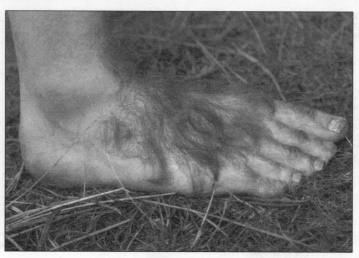

～10～

FILMING THE FILMS

It looks a bit like a comic book. The big, bulky binder is filled with hundreds of pages divided into 'frames' containing thumb-nail sketches of all the scenes in the film. This is a 'storyboard' and this is where the real filming of *The Lord of the Rings* began.

The storyboard was invented years ago by movie cartoonists to work out the gags in their pictures before starting the animation. Later, live-action film directors started using the method to plan their movies; Peter Jackson began *The Lord of the Rings* project by making a storyboard of all three movies. With the help of a couple of artists, the script was turned into a picture-strip version of the story, which Peter would refer to on many occasions during filming.

Next, they made an 'animatic'. This is a filmed version of the still drawings on the storyboard, photographed in sequence, with a soundtrack made up of the 'dialogue' (the characters' lines in the script), music and sound-effects.

Watching an animatic gives the director a rough idea of what the finished film will look like. Simple computer animations were also made for one or two of those sequences that would involve a lot of special effects, such as Gandalf's battle with the Balrog.

"The animatic," says Peter, "is a real help in planning the shooting of the actual movie: you immediately get an idea whether the story is right and whether the characters are working." Only when Peter was happy with the way in which the films were coming together, did the cameras roll.

For the next fourteen months, time seemed to stand still. Day after day, week after week, the cast and crew battled with the weather and against time to get three long movies 'in the can'.

All three films were being shot alongside one another and that is a 'first'. On one day they might be filming an opening scene from *The Fellowship of the Ring* and, next day, shooting the final scenes from the third film, *The Return of the King*.

Orcs get ready to shoot a scene

"In the past," explains Peter, "film trilogies have always been an original movie followed by two sequels, usually with some of the same characters, but completely new stories. What we've done is tell *one story* over the space of three films, and that's unique."

The Lord of the Rings was such a big project that while Peter was directing the key scenes, as many as four or five other film units might be filming different sequences, often on different locations several miles away. With the help of satellite hookups, Peter was able to film his scenes *and* keep an eye on what the other units were doing!

Amazingly, he never seems to have lost his way. "I simply tried to forget the idea that it's three movies," he says. "I treated it as one big story with

Peter Jackson reviewing shots on location

lots of scenes; fortunately, I know exactly where every one of those scenes goes within the story!"

Like most films, there were unexpected mishaps. Travelling to so many places around the two islands of New Zealand, trekking into woods and deserts and struggling up mountains, meant that the film crew ran into all kinds of weather. They were snowed in, washed out and, on one very windy day, came back from shooting to find that the large tent, that was the actors' dressing-room, had just blown away!

When it got very wet, the hobbits had to be given piggy-back rides from the location sets by members of the crew so that the actors didn't get their hobbit feet bogged down in the mud!

There was a handful of accidents, including one or two that might have turned out to be a lot more serious than they actually were. Sean Astin, playing Sam, seems to have had more than his fair share. One day, he was eating lunch on the Rivendell set, when a huge wooden loom (used for making tapestries) fell down, hit him on the head and knocked him out! Sean was rushed to hospital for an X-ray but, fortunately, no serious damage had been done. For several days afterwards, his fellow hobbit-actors would make him jump by pointing behind him and shouting: "Loom!"

Rather more serious was the accident that happened when they were filming the scene at the end of *The Fellowship of the Ring,* in which Sam rushes into the river after the departing boat containing the invisible Frodo.

Sam wading after Frodo's boat

Sean leapt excitedly down the bank, splashed into the water and gave a sudden yelp of pain. He had trodden on a piece of tree branch sticking up from the river-bed that had pierced not only his hobbit foot but also his *own* foot. When the rubber foot was cut away in order to see what damage had been done, there was so much blood that a helicopter was sent for, to air-lift Sean to hospital.

There were a number of mishaps with horses: stunt-double Kirin Shah had to jump off a

Arwen on horseback

speeding pony when it suddenly decided to bolt, and various other riders lost their horses or bumped into trees! The least expected accident happened when Tolkien artist Alan Lee fell off the edge of one of the sets and broke his arm – fortunately not the one he uses for drawing!

Viggo Mortensen, who plays Aragorn and who insisted on doing his own stunts, got hurt several times. "That's what happens," he explains, "when you throw yourself into things! Aragorn is the most physical character in the story. He leads by example and his physical courage or recklessness, depending on how you look at it, is what gets him through life."

Sword in hand: Viggo Mortensen as Aragorn

For Viggo, it was also part of the experience of telling this particular story. "*The Lord of the Rings* is about a long journey," he says. "The main characters are meant to be cold and tired and wet. It's a journey with mud, rain and snow — all the things that *we* have experienced in making the film! So, hopefully, it ought to look legitimate!"

Elijah Wood agrees: "It's been such a wonderful adventure. We were working hard and going everywhere and it actually felt, in some ways, very much like the adventure that takes place in the film."

❧ 11 ❧

SPECIAL EFFECTS

The Lord of the Rings is rather like a magic show –
full of illusions. And, like a magic show, it's not
always easy to know what's real and what's not!

As Richard Taylor of Weta Workshop explains:
"As long as you keep changing the way you do
things, the audience will find it very difficult to
work out how the tricks are being done!"

The film trilogy features just about every trick
in the cinema special-effects book. To create the
illusion that the hobbits are small characters, the
film-makers use what is called 'forced perspective'.
This is how it works: Elijah Wood as Frodo and
Ian McKellen as Gandalf seem to be sitting talking
to one another, but Gandalf is really much nearer
to the camera than Frodo, which makes him
appear larger.

Frodo and Gandalf face to face in 'forced perspective'

The trick works because the camera doesn't 'see' the gap between the actors and they look as if they are face to face and the correct size for their characters. Acting in scenes like this can be hard because the actors can hear each other's lines, but are never actually looking at one another!

The films also use 'blue-screen' techniques. Actors are filmed in front of a blue screen; then, using a process which treats all blue areas on film as if they are transparent, those shots are combined with filmed or painted backgrounds.

For example, there is a sequence in *The*

Fellowship of the Ring in which Frodo and his companions visit Lothlórien and stand looking out across the city among the trees. In fact, they were filmed looking at a blue screen; the view was added later using film shot on an elaborate miniature set.

Many films have used scale models, but few will equal those built for *The Lord of the Rings*.

Among the scale sets in the first film are the orc-pits deep beneath the tower at Orthanc, and the figures of the Argonath (huge stone statues of Aragorn's ancestors) which the Fellowship pass on the River Anduin.

Scale model of Rivendell

As well as fantastical places, the films feature a number of scary creatures and characters. There are the terrible Ringwraiths, who are first seen as nine faceless riders cloaked in tattered black robes, galloping in pursuit of Frodo and his friends. Later, when Frodo puts on the Ring, he sees the deadly Ringwraiths as they really are (see page 56).

Among the monsters featured in the first film is the slimy Watcher in the Water, which grabs at the companions with its long, snake-like tentacles. There are more dangerous encounters inside the mountain city of Moria, where the travellers battle an army of scuttling goblins and a huge cave-troll, before facing the monstrous Balrog that rises out of the depths on wings of fire!

Tolkien's monsters have been brought to life at Weta Digital, an associate company of Weta Workshop, by a team of over two hundred talented animators using computers.

In the four years before filming began, some amazing processes were developed to assist the animators. The most staggering is a computer programme using a 'behavioural simulation system'; with this, whole armies can be created on a computer screen, and every single soldier can be programmed with the 'brains' to make choices about how to fight in battle — or even run away!

Also making occasional appearances are digital versions of the some of the film's human, hobbit, dwarf and elf characters. The real actors were filmed wearing 'motion-capture suits'. The cameras recorded how the actors moved, then converted those moves into digital information that was used to create computer-generated actors who could do things quite impossible for their flesh-and-blood doubles.

This system will be used to create the most famous creature-character in Tolkien's story: Gollum, who will be seen for the first time in *The Two Towers*. Introduced in *The Hobbit*, it was Gollum who kept the One Ring hidden for many years, until the day on which it was found by Bilbo Baggins. In *The Lord of the Rings,* we discover

The gleam of the Ring falls on Frodo

exactly how Gollum came by the Ring and learn what part he has to play in its future.

Although the movie trilogy will be full of all kinds of special effects, from the dramatic wizard's duel between Gandalf and Saruman, to the mysterious inscription that magically appears on the Ring's surface, it is first and foremost a story about people – their hopes and fears, their courage and treachery, their daring and cowardice.

However many moments there are in the films when we gasp and find ourselves on the edge of our seats, Peter Jackson knows that it won't matter how breathtaking the effects are if we don't care about those characters.

~ 12 ~

THE JOURNEY CONTINUES...

Years and years of work, and still Peter Jackson's film trilogy, *The Lord of the Rings*, isn't finished!

Although, at long last, the first of those films, *The Fellowship of the Ring*, has reached the world's cinema screens, a lot of people are still busily working on the next two pictures, *The Two Towers* and *The Return of the King*, editing scenes and adding music and special effects.

It will be another two years before movie-goers will have seen the finished trilogy, but Peter hopes that, long before then, audiences will begin to understand just how much thought, imagination, hard work and love is going into completing this ambitious project.

"These films," he says, "are being made *by* fans of the book, *for* fans of the book! As for people who *haven't* read *The Lord of the Rings*, I think that, in seeing the films, they will experience something of the excitement and magic that is to be found in Tolkien's book."

Two years is a long time to wait if you want to know how the story ends! In the meantime, of course, you *could* do what the young Peter Jackson did, many years ago – pick up a copy of the original book and discover for yourself one of the most unusual and unforgettable tales ever told...